THE CRYING MOUNTAIN

A MEXICAN LEGEND

RETOLD BY PATRICIA ALMADA
ILLUSTRATED BY CHRISTINA GONZÁLEZ

Rigby

© 1997 by Rigby,
a division of Reed Elsevier Inc.
1000 Hart Rd.
Barrington, IL 60010-2627

05 04 03
10 9 8 7

Printed in Singapore

ISBN 0-7635-3220-7

M̲any years ago in ancient Mexico, a little
princess was born. Her father, the Toltec king, was
filled with joy. "My daughter will be wise and kind. She
will marry a Toltec noble, and she will become queen of
our people when I die," he announced proudly.

The young princess—who was named Ixtaccihuatl, or Ixta for short—did not disappoint her father. Even as a child, she had a thirst for knowledge.

"Just like a true Toltec!" remarked the king. He ordered the best tutors in the kingdom to the palace so they could teach Ixta all that she needed to know.

Ixta learned how pyramids were built from master builders. She learned about the planting of corn, squash, beans, and cotton from expert farmers. And she learned to sculpt monuments in stone like the best artisans. From the weavers, she learned the patterns and designs of her people. From the astronomers, she learned to watch the skies for the cycles of time.

As the years passed, Ixta was no longer satisfied to learn from tutors in the palace. She wanted to see for herself the splendors of the empire. At first, her father was afraid to let her leave the palace grounds because some of the neighboring peoples, like the Chichimecas, were often at war with the Toltecs.

"But father," insisted Ixta, "the people must know me, and I must know them. Besides, there is so much more I must learn before I become their ruler."

The king was afraid for her safety, but he was also anxious to please his daughter. So he agreed to let her explore the empire. The traveling party was soon assembled. The king said good-bye to his daughter and embraced her with tears in his eyes.

Word spread quickly through the empire that Princess Ixta was traveling. As she approached each village, the people hurried to welcome her. It was unusual for a Toltec princess to be among the people, so everyone was most curious to meet her.

Ixta was easy to find, even when surrounded by her guards, because she always wore flowing white dresses embroidered with colorful royal designs. Her long black hair was neatly braided into thick braids, and she wore lovely gold jewelry.

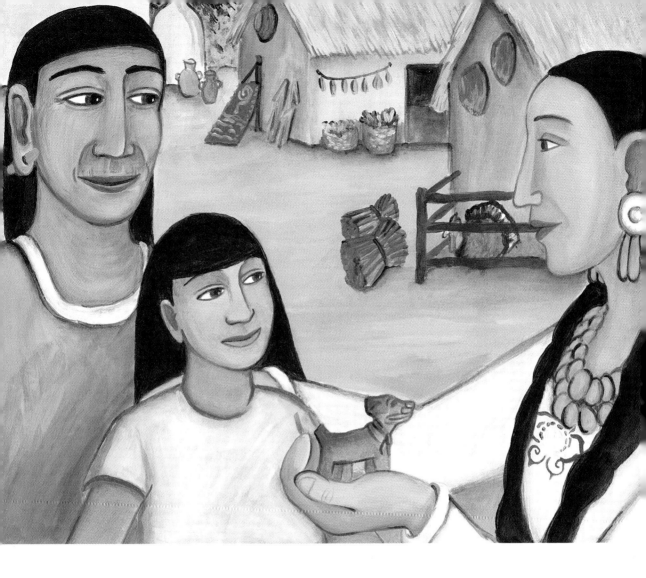

Ixta spent long hours talking to the people, young and old. She listened to stories of long ago, watched artisans at work, and visited temples, quarries, marketplaces, farmer's fields, and homes. She gave small gifts to everyone she met, and the people were impressed by her kindness, compassion, and beauty.

Ixta, in turn, was taken by the vastness and beauty of the empire. The green forests, sparkling lakes, and majestic mountains were even more beautiful than she had imagined. Early one morning, Ixta was awakened by her guards, who had spotted a group of Chichimecan warriors approaching their camp.

This was cause for great concern because the Chichimecas, a neighboring people, were often at war with the Toltecs. They soon found out that the Chichimecan warriors were only escorting their prince, Popocatepetl, as he passed through the Toltec empire. "I would like to meet Princess Ixta and pay my respects. I have heard of her wisdom and beauty," said the prince.

Ixta agreed to meet with Popo—as he was called for short—under the watchful eyes of her guards. The young prince was strong and handsome. He wore a jaguar-skin cape around his shoulders and the finest quetzal feathers on his headdress.

"The Chichimecas are skilled hunters, and the Toltecs are master builders," he said as they walked along the riverbank. "Our people can learn much from each other."

They spoke for hours, and Ixta realized that she had fallen in love with the handsome Chichimecan prince. As the sun was setting behind the snowcapped mountains, Popo asked Ixta to become his wife.

"My father would never allow me to marry you," Ixta answered sadly. "My duty is to marry a Toltec noble, but my heart will always be yours." And Ixta returned to the palace, knowing she would probably never see Popo again.

As the years passed, Ixta's father was growing weaker with age and was anxious for his daughter to marry. He could not understand why Ixta had refused all her suitors. "It is time for you to marry, my beautiful daughter," he said one day. "I will ask the Toltec nobles to gather so you may choose the one who will become your husband."

When Popo was informed of this news, he decided to see the king at once. Dressed in his finest royal garments and bearing many gifts, he respectfully asked for Ixta's hand in marriage. He spoke of their meeting years ago and of Ixta's love for him.

"My daughter will marry only a Toltec noble. The Chichimecas are a backward people who live in caves and make wars against us!" shouted the king. Then he ordered Popo to be removed from the palace grounds forever.

Princess Ixta was saddened but not surprised at her father's words, for she knew of his hatred of the Chichimecas. However, she still loved Popo and refused to choose a Toltec husband, hoping that her father would change his mind.

Month after month, her father asked her to choose a Toltec husband. Each time, she refused. Soon Ixta understood that her father would never change his mind and lost all desire to live.

She became ill with grief and would not eat or speak. The best healers and priests were summoned to the palace. Rich offerings were given to the gods of the sun and the moon, but even then Ixta grew weaker each day. Finally the king became afraid that his daughter would die of a broken heart and decided to send messengers in search of Popo.

When Popo heard the message, he rushed to Ixta's side. As he approached the palace, he realized that the people were in mourning. There was silence in the streets, the pathways leading to the castle were lined with the orange flowers of the dead, and wailing could be heard inside the palace walls. The beautiful Ixta, beloved princess of the Toltec empire, was already dead.

"My love will bring her back," whispered Popo as he gently lifted the princess and carried her out of the palace. In the street, a long procession formed as the people followed Popo through the cool forest and into the countryside.

Popo ordered an enormous pyramid built on the very same spot where he had first seen Ixta. Thousands of people worked all day in complete silence. When the sun shone its last rays, the pyramid was finally done.

Popo climbed to the top and carefully laid Ixta to rest. Then he built a fire of sweet-smelling pine needles and waited for a sign of life. The black smoke rose slowly to the sky, and sadness covered the land as the news of Ixta's death spread.

After many days, a saddened Popocatepetl came down from the pyramid. The people recognized his royal robes, but his appearance was changed. Popo's hair was gray, and his shoulders were rounded with the burden of his grief.

He now realized that he could not bring Ixta back to life and ordered that an even larger pyramid be built to the south of the first one. As soon as it was completed, Popo bid farewell to his people and climbed to the top. There he stayed, forever guarding the resting place of his beloved Ixta.

The snows came, and with the passing of the years, the pyramids became volcanoes. In the outskirts of Mexico City, two beautiful snowcapped volcanoes still frame the valley. The quiet one is named Ixtaccihuatl, which means Sleeping Woman. The taller one is Popocatepetl, the Crying Mountain. It often rumbles and shakes, spewing out white smoke.

To this the storytellers say, "There goes Popo again, crying for his sweetheart."